The ARTS

DESIGN

Catherine McDermott

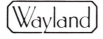
Wayland

The Arts

Architecture
Cinema
Dance
Design
Literature
Music
Painting and Sculpture
Photography
Theatre

Cover illustration: This prototype of the Jaguar XJ220 was unveiled at the 1988 International Motor Show in Birmingham, Britain. Its bodywork, using the latest developments in aerodynamics and motor technology, is made from bonded aluminium, which combines a sleek appearance with lightness and strength.

Book Editor: Tracey Smith
Series Editor: Rosemary Ashley
Designer: David Armitage

First published in 1989 by
Wayland (Publishers) Limited
61 Western Road, Hove
East Sussex BN3 1JD, England

© Copyright 1989 Wayland (Publishers) Ltd.

British Library Cataloguing in Publication Data
McDermott, Catherine
   Design. – (The Arts).
   1. Design
   I. Title   II. Series
   745.4

ISBN 1–85210–454–6

Typeset by DP Press, Sevenoaks, England
Printed and bound in Italy

Contents

1 Introduction to Design

All the things we use in everyday life, from soft-drink cans to hamburger packs, have been designed. Someone has chosen the material, colour and shape, and made key decisions about the way such ordinary objects in our world actually look. It is a fact that the modern society in which most of us live is a completely designed environment.

Many of the inventions that we take for granted in the types of lifestyle we lead are the result of important industrial changes in the nineteenth century. The invention of mass-production techniques provided people with standardized goods for the first time. Sales, advertising and retailing techniques were developed to cater for the new consumer society. One familiar example of selling a particular product on an international scale is the success of the American company Coca-Cola: there must be very few places in the world where it is not possible to buy this drink, packaged with its distinctive graphic logo.

Below *Hill House, near Glasgow in Scotland, was built by Charles Rennie Mackintosh (1868–1928). All the distinctive furniture and decoration he designed still remains and the house attracts visitors from all over the world. It represents a unique survival from one of the most admired architects of the twentieth century.*

Above *This Coca-Cola advertisement dates from 1941 and demonstrates the superior importance of illustration over photography as an advertising technique at this time. American products such as this were soon to dominate world markets and reinforce the economic strength of the United States.*

The following chapters discuss the development of design from the Industrial Revolution of the eighteenth and nineteenth centuries, and set out to explain how new theories and ideas have affected the developed Western world.

Design as a way of shaping an object, however, is a much older concept. Early primitive societies shaped flint for tools and developed symbolic painted images to interpret their cultures. Australian Aboriginal and North American Indian life still celebrates some of these achievements and reminds us that early civilizations developed superb craftsmanship and decorative skills.

In the museums of the world's larger cities one can see some fine collections of ancient art. From these, we can assess the achievement of Egyptian tomb painters, the technique of Roman glass-making and the skills used by the makers of Greek ceramic vases, for example. Objects like these continue to inspire and influence design.

The production of goods in Ancient Egypt and the Classical world was based on traditional craft techniques. A craft worker would be responsible for the complete production of an object. The potter, for example, would normally dig the clay, prepare it and throw it, then decorate, glaze and fire the pot.

Centuries later, during the Middle Ages, craft workers organized themselves into guilds, which operated rather like present-day trade

unions, to protect their members. Such creative activities, however, were not given the same status as the fine-art genres of painting and sculpture. The concept of formal art education, which had begun during the Renaissance, confirmed this imbalance.

The famous French Beaux Arts education system of the nineteenth century operated a hierarchy which put painting first and design last. The same teaching pattern was copied throughout Europe and remained virtually unchanged until after the Second World War (1939–45). Such deep rooted traditions proved difficult to change and it is only recently that society has come to revise its views.

The shift from small-scale craft production to the modern ideas of marketing and design can be traced back to the Industrial Revolution of the eighteenth century. Cheaper printing techniques helped to spread ideas and, for the first time, books about design were published. One of the most famous of these was a catalogue of furniture designs by Thomas Chippendale, published in London in 1754 and called *The Director*. This book contained engraved illustrations of exotic and fashionable furniture and it also marked an important turning point for design. Publications like this suggested that designers were no longer simple rural craftsmen but sophisticated businessmen. Chippendale, for example, was both a talented designer and an entrepreneur; he ran his design practice from Covent Garden, in the heart of London. His clients were amongst the most prestigious in the land and surviving business correspondence suggests he had social and intellectual ambitions of the highest order. Chippendale's approach marked a much wider change.

Britain was at the centre of important new attitudes to design. Clubs and societies were formed by enlightened young industrialists, one of the most distinguished of these pioneer manufacturers being Josiah Wedgwood (1730–95). Wedgwood did not publish his ideas on design, but through surviving letters it is possible to analyze one of the prototype industries of the Industrial Revolution.

Left *Thomas Chippendale (c. 1718–79) was one of the most important furniture designers of the eighteenth century. His catalogue,* The Director, *suggested a new status for architects, designers and consumers.*

Far left *This cabinet was designed by William Benson, a member of the British Arts and Crafts Movement. It is shown here in the old Dining Rooms of the Victoria and Albert Museum in London, which were decorated by William Morris. Details such as the elaborate metal hinges on the cabinet highlight the nineteenth century's admiration of mediaeval art and design.*

Below *This tableware was produced by Wedgwood during the 1980s, but the shapes used originated in Josiah Wedgwood's factory over two hundred years ago.*

Above *This table by Ettore Sottsass is part of a collection produced by the Memphis group. Outrageous furniture such as this, using plastic laminates and bold colours, made the group's designs famous. Their work can also be described as being part of the new Post-Modernist style of the 1980s.*

Far Right *This staircase detail from the 1930s reveals the superb sculptural effects that Modernist architects sought to achieve.*

In 1759, Wedgwood inherited the family ceramic business in Staffordshire and set about reforming it. During the years of the 1760s and 1770s, he set out ground rules for industrial production that were copied all over the world. At his factory in Staffordshire he introduced steam power, and broke down the process of production into separate activities. This principle is called the division of labour. This was a simple but profound change which upturned the tradition that individual workers controlled the complete process of production; instead each worker specialized in one small activity. Wedgwood also used systematic scientific-research methods in his factory and was one of the first manufacturers to use newspaper advertising. His approach to marketing and business was far in advance of his contemporaries and reflected the new economic theories of the age, which had been put forward in books such as Adam Smith's *The Wealth of Nations*, published in 1776.

These new inventions, theories and techniques developed in Britain at the end of the eighteenth century. Their introduction has become known as the Industrial Revolution. The age of steam power, the engineering advances, the development of the factory system and a rapid population growth were the factors that changed British society for ever. We are still living with the effects of these changes and we are trying to come to terms with their implications. This book sets out to show how the work of designers was, in turn, influenced by these events.

② High Victorian Design

Below inset *This textile print commemorates the Great Exhibition of 1851. Organized by Prince Albert, it was an outstanding success, showing the latest in technology and attracting millions of visitors.*

In 1851, the British decided to stage a prestigious international exhibition of design, and a site was chosen in Hyde Park, in the centre of London. The building that was constructed for the exhibition became world famous. The architect, Joseph Paxton, built it of glass and iron panels, and it was designed to demonstrate the latest industrial techniques and materials. It was immediately nicknamed the Crystal Palace. The Great Exhibition of 1851 proved immensely popular and turned out to be a celebration of the new technology and inventions of the Industrial Revolution. The exhibition included products from India, the United States and many other countries.

Below *This hand-coloured print shows the American section of the Great Exhibition. Objects and machines from all over the world were displayed and the exhibition's success encouraged the United States to organize trade fairs along the same lines.*

Above *This reconstructed Victorian parlour gives us some idea of nineteenth century taste. Victorians preferred rooms to look cluttered, with dark colours and lots of ornaments.*

Right *The Prince Albert chair is now in the collection of the Victoria and Albert Museum in London, but it was orginally shown in the Great Exhibition of 1851. The design is typical of its period.*

A lavish hand-coloured catalogue from the exhibition has survived, illustrating the products of this new age. A hundred and forty years later, however, a great deal of what was admired then is now difficult to appreciate. Popular High-Victorian design was confident, large-scale and ornate. Furniture was extravagantly carved and the newly developed techniques of upholstery encouraged the production of deeply-padded sofas and chairs. Interiors favoured complicated patterned wallpapers in shades of rich green and maroon. These were chosen with the simple practical reason in mind that the open coal-fires of Victorian homes gave out much dirt and smoke.

Right *Owen Jones'* Grammar of Ornament, *first published in 1856, was the most important source book for nineteenth-century designers. It attempted to provide an encyclopaedic survey of historical ornament and contained examples of both eastern and western design motifs. Shown here is a sample page of Egyptian designs.*

In the nineteenth century, the movement of people from the countryside to the new industrial towns encouraged a population explosion, and the demand for new products expanded rapidly, even among the poor. At the same time, the new pioneers of the United States had set out to colonize the West. To cater for consumer needs, mail-order catalogues appeared, illustrating goods for sale. American manufacturers used all the techniques of present-day salesmanship, including advertising, and they recognized that good design would boost sales and, as such, improve the nation's prosperity.

In the 1840s, Britain, like many other countries, decided to launch a national programme of design schools to educate designers for industry. The most famous of these institutions was the South Kensington School in London, later attached to the Victoria and Albert Museum. Here, designers were taught to draw and to learn about ornament. Many of the important teachers published books which became the standard sources of information. An example of these is a book by Owen Jones called *The Grammar of Ornament*. This book set out page after page of coloured illustrations of decoration from all over the world. Egyptian, South American, Indian and Chinese sources were all included. These pages provided the source materials which nineteenth-century designers used to decorate textiles, interiors, tiles, railway stations, market halls and homes. This pulling together of ideas from the past and all kinds of different cultures is called eclecticism and it is a part of the reason why nineteenth-century design is so rich and varied in its appearance.

The nineteenth century saw the development of the modern consumer society, with cheaper mass-produced goods becoming more widely available. Design became a subject of great interest. Magazines with titles like *The Universal Decorator* appeared, and books such as Charles Eastlake's *Hints on Household Taste*, ran to six editions in New York alone.

Independent industrial designers now began to appear on the scene. One of these, Christopher Dresser (1834–1904), published a whole series of books on design. Dresser's highly individual approach to the subject attracted a lot of interest from famous manufacturers of his time; Elkington's of Sheffield, for example, which specialized in the production of silver plate, and Doulton's, which manufactured tiles for the department store Liberty's of London. Dresser was a significant figure because he is an early example of a designer who was commissioned to create new designs specifically to boost sales for a company.

While these changes in production and sales were taking place, many critics were worried by shoddy standards and over-elaborate designs flooding the new areas of growth. Heated debates took place about which decoration was considered appropriate for which particular market; and some of the most talented designers simply rejected the mass-production system and looked for inspiration from traditional hand-worked crafts.

Left *The development of modern advertising began in the nineteenth century, when mass-produced goods were sold under a brand name for the first time. Nineteenth-century advertising techniques now seem crude, but their methods are not that far removed from present-day television advertising.*

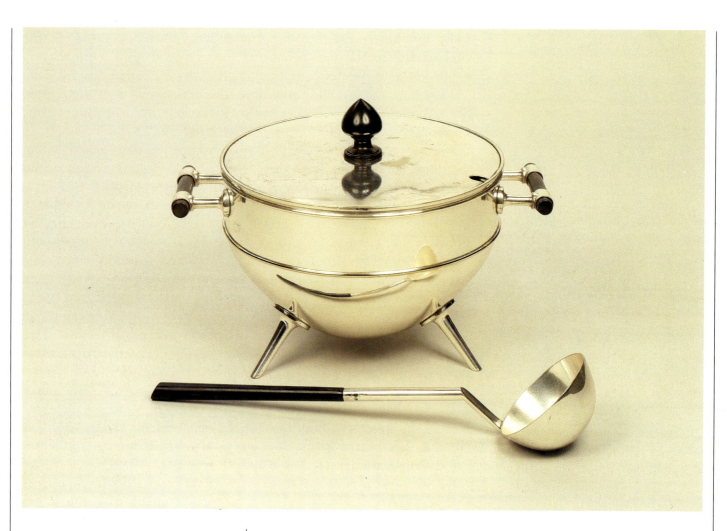

The Arts and Crafts Movement this inspired is discussed in the following chapter. Contrary to the ideals behind this movement, however, manufacturers later appropriated these designs into the factories. It is not without a certain sense of irony that when we look at late nineteenth-century products, we can see that a number of them used machine techniques to imitate the effect of hand production. The hammer marks of the silversmith, for example, were copied by machine and the abstract effects of simple potter's glazes were mechanically produced.

Something of these different approaches to design can be seen in the nineteenth century's last great decorative movement, Art Nouveau (meaning 'New Art'). This French term is extremely apt as it was Paris that was to become the centre of this movement. Art Nouveau was inspired by the natural curving forms of plants and flowers. One of its best-known designers was Hector Guimard (1867–1942), who created the sumptuous swirling bronze entrances to the Paris Metro stations that have become classic examples of the Art Nouveau style. The influence of Art Nouveau was international and it can be seen in many famous objects such as Tiffany glass; generally these pieces were unique and individually produced, but their stylistic influence filtered down to a mass market.

3 Arts and Crafts Ideals

In the last chapter, the new materials and forms which made Victorian design so distinctive were discussed. These expressed the vigorous spirit of an age that we can still recognize and admire.

Britain was the first country to experience the effects of the Industrial Revolution and the nineteenth century was a period of dramatic social and economic change. The Victorians were the first to make products for a new mass market but there were problems with the quality and design of these goods. At the same time that markets were expanding, many important designers and architects were worried about the radical changes they saw all around them. They saw the Industrial Revolution only in terms of large ugly cities, pollution and slum housing. These critics felt that the traditional values of life were in danger of being destroyed by industrial progress and change. They believed that lessons to be learnt from the past could improve the quality of life and the visual appearance of ordinary objects in the home. This new spirit of anti-industrialization quickly found a name and became known as the Arts and Crafts Movement.

Below *William Morris (1834–96) dedicated his life to improving the quality of design. He founded his Kelmscott Press in 1890, with the aim of raising the standards of book design and printing. He took a special interest in graphic design and the appearance of printed matter, using his own typefaces and decorative borders, which were reminiscent of the illuminated manuscripts of the Middle Ages.*

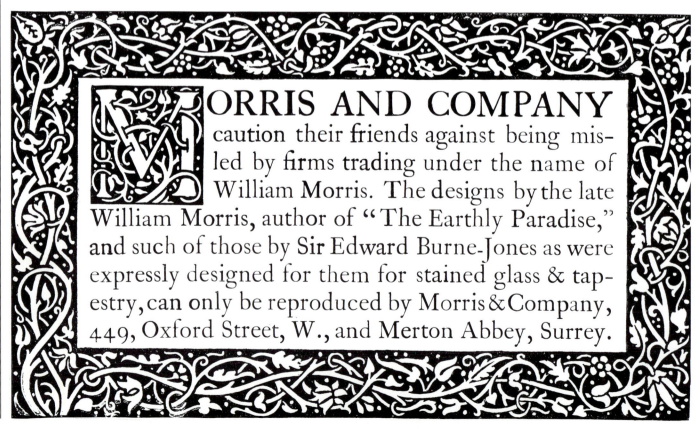

MORRIS AND COMPANY caution their friends against being misled by firms trading under the name of William Morris. The designs by the late William Morris, author of "The Earthly Paradise," and such of those by Sir Edward Burne-Jones as were expressly designed for them for stained glass & tapestry, can only be reproduced by Morris & Company, 449, Oxford Street, W., and Merton Abbey, Surrey.

Although its origins were British, as a stylistic influence, Arts and Crafts values spread throughout Europe and the United States. It is worth bearing in mind now, when you watch television advertisements, go shopping, or simply look around your own home, that many of the objects you are familiar with owe a debt to a way of thinking about design that was developed by the Arts and Crafts Movement in the nineteenth century.

The Arts and Craft Movement was an instinctive reaction against the very visible effects of the Industrial Revolution, and it happened almost immediately. A well-known example of the kind of protest made came as early as 1836, from the Victorian architect Augustus Welby Pugin (1812–52). In that year he published a book called *Contrasts* which contained a very simple message; Pugin believed that the mediaeval past, which he called Gothic, showed more understanding of beauty and design than the contemporary architecture of the nineteenth century. *Contrasts* used simple examples to illustrate his point of view. The caring treatment of the sick in a beautiful fifteenth-century monastery, for example, is contrasted with the notorious Victorian workhouses so vividly described in Charles Dickens' novels.

Pugin went on to make the same kind of comment about the field of design. For him, Gothic, from both a moral and visual point of view, was the only style in which to work. The best place to see the results of his theories is the Houses of Parliament in London, which were rebuilt in the 1830s after a disastrous fire. Pugin was given the job of designing all the decoration, furniture, tiles, wallpaper and textiles in the Gothic style. Nearly all of this work survives today.

The Houses of Parliament suggested the possibilities of using the Gothic style not only for churches but also for civil life. This style proved immensely successful, so much so that Pugin's work made a deep impression on his contemporaries, and the Gothic style was discovered and exploited as a key element in Victorian architecture. We can identify many famous buildings in the style, including Harvard University in Cambridge, Massachusetts, and St Pancras Station, London. Influenced by Pugin's beliefs, other designers and critics began to think about the mediaeval past as a way of achieving social reform through design.

Without a doubt, the most important of these designers was William Morris (1834–96). Despising the greedy values of capitalism and profit that could destroy the quality of people's lives, he became a designer, writer and a committed socialist. William Morris came to be one of the most influential thinkers of his generation, and his ideas remain important to this day.

In 1862, disillusioned with the products he saw on sale, Morris set up his own design company. It has since become associated with one basic idea, the concept of truth to materials. Morris, and many other design reformers, believed that every material has its own value; for example, the natural colour of wood or the glaze of a well-made pot.

Above *William Morris remains one of the most important and charismatic figures of the nineteenth century. He directed his energies towards social reform, literature and politics as well as design. Morris' books were read world-wide and were regarded as standard texts well into the twentieth century. The life and works of William Morris represent a sensible starting point for anyone who is interested in the history of industrial design.*

Above right *William Morris' company Morris & Co., founded in 1861, marketed a number of chairs among its furniture designs. Most of these used simple traditional forms, which were upholstered with Morris fabric. This design is more elaborate than most, but remains true to Morris' ideals and is a satisfying and functional piece.*

Morris believed that these qualities had to be respected in every design. He tried to revive traditional methods of craft production that had been taken over by new industrial processes. One example of this is in the dyeing of cloth. In the early nineteenth century, the chemical industry developed the first synthetic dyes, including new bright purples and yellows which Morris hated. At his own print works in Surrey, England, Morris revived the use of traditional vegetable dyes used in craft techniques, which produced such colours as the distinctive blue of indigo.

Morris spent hours at the Victoria and Albert Museum in London, researching naturalistic patterns from sources as varied as the English Tudor period and Islamic cultures. He admired the traditional forms that had developed over the centuries rather than those designed by a single individual. These forms were called vernacular and they reflected a slow process of artistic evolution that the Arts and Crafts designers deeply admired.

The wallpapers, textiles and furniture Morris designed from 1860 to his death in 1896 were immensely popular during his lifetime and have remained so until the present day. Although he never realized his ambition to produce his designs cheaply, his new approach to design stimulated a whole generation of designers. By the end of the nineteenth century, Britain was the most influential country in the world for new design ideas. Countries as far apart as Japan and the United States sent designers to Britain to study this innovative work.

British design magazines such as *The Studio* attracted many international subscribers. There are many important names to consider here, but perhaps the best known is the Glasgow architect, Charles Rennie Mackintosh (1868–1928). His distinctive black-and-white designs have made him one of the world's best-known designers, and the influence of his work is widespread. It is also fair to say that the small-scale individual production of designers such as Mackintosh and Morris did have some impact on industrial production.

DRINK·TO·ME·ONLY·WITH·THINE·EYES

Above inset *Walter Crane was a famous Victorian illustrator and the romantic and elaborate design of this example is typical of his style. Crane and many of his contemporaries were fond of using historical subject matter for their illustrations.*

Right *This illustration was produced in 1900 by Kate Greenaway for a children's songbook. The Victorians admired sentimental images of childhood; the children in this picture are certainly pretty, but they are not completely realistic.*

Victorian commercial publishers, for example, tried to raise their standards by commissioning creative illustrators. Two well-known examples were Kate Greenaway and Walter Crane. The Victorians found design a stimulating subject for debate, and the search for new values resulted in other interesting developments.

In 1896, an Arts and Crafts architect, called Charles Robert Ashbee (1863–1925), took one hundred workmen from London's East End to Chipping Campden, a small village in the Cotswold hills in England. This was a social experiment and the workmen tried to produce beautiful objects in an appropriate romantic and rural setting. The Guild of Handicrafts, as it was called, became very famous, and although it finally went bankrupt, its influence extended far beyond the small scale of its activities.

Throughout the twentieth century, Ashbee's dream of country living has been kept alive by generations of distinguished craftspeople. In every part of the developed world, creative individuals, depressed by the thought of ever-increasing industrialization, have opted to seek out a rural idyll and dedicate themselves to craft work.

This movement has effectively split design and craft activity, and in the 1980s the two words have come to mean very different things. Design is generally associated with manufacturing, industry and commerce, while craft is associated with expensive, individually-made products.

Some countries have tried to combine the two strands. The Scandinavian countries, with their small populations and plentiful natural resources, are an example of this attempt. During the 1930s, the famous Finnish architect Alvar Aalto (1898–1976) successfully integrated craft ideals with the modern production methods used in the manufacture of his furniture.

The debate that so concerned the Victorians, hand-crafting versus machine production, and the purpose and function of design, remains controversial. The image encouraged by the Arts and Crafts Movement is a rather romantic view of cornfields, country cottages and picturesque villages. As a counterbalance to the increasing 'high-tech' quality of present-day living, the crafts have come to represent an alternative lifestyle. This move towards a simpler way of living was explored by the hippy culture that grew up around California in the late 1960s.

In the late twentieth century, the real impact of the Arts and Crafts Movement has been diverted into mainstream mass-produced design. The same people who buy home computers and microwave ovens also buy country-look pine kitchens and floral-print curtains, which have more than a touch of William Morris in their design. During the 1970s and the 1980s, British retailers such as Laura Ashley and Terence Conran's Habitat Stores made this style their hallmark. The visual impact of the Arts and Crafts Movement remains an enduring influence on design. Its nostalgic image has remained popular to the present day.

Below *Laura Ashley, photographed here in her own home, founded an international chain of highly influential shops. The look she created was traditional and homely and her fabrics and wallpapers have found favour with millions of customers worldwide.*

4 The Modern Movement

One of the most important changes in twentieth-century design was a response to the First World War (1914–18). This cruel conflict, with its massive loss of young lives, brought with it important political and social change and helped to alter the way people thought about themselves and society.

Loss and devastation on such a huge scale had a long-lasting effect, yet it inspired optimism about a new future in which design and

Above *Le Corbusier's chapel at Ronchamps, France, represents a departure from his geometric, white architectural style. The roof profile creates a dramatic effect and contrasts strongly with the form of the bell tower.*

technology would both play an important part. After all, the century had begun with a whole series of inventions that were about to change everyday life forever. The first aircraft and motor cars appeared, the telephone transformed communications, and mass entertainment developed with the first silent movies. The world seemed an exciting and challenging place, and everywhere there was a tremendous interest in experimentation and a belief in a new technological future.

In the early years of the century this spirit of the modern influenced all the visual arts. The Cubist Movement, developed during the early 1900s by the painters Pablo Picasso and Georges Braque, changed the whole naturalistic approach of European painting that had developed since the Renaissance in the sixteenth century.

At the same time, architects and designers were attempting to exploit new techniques and building methods. They were looking for equally revolutionary forms with which to express their ideas. In the 1930s, the Swiss architect, Le Corbusier (1887–1965) experimented with pure white concrete forms. He created houses which he described as 'machines for living in'. In New York the first high-rise buildings were being built. Everywhere there was talk of machines and change.

Designers also responded to these challenges, and the years following the First World War were highly stimulating and creative. This period of design has become known as the Modern Movement.

The search for what was termed Modernism was international, but each country produced its own version of this style and responded to the challenge in an individual way. Russia is a very good example of this. In 1917 the country, which for centuries had been ruled by an autocracy, had undergone a violent revolution, resulting in the Tsar's execution and exile for the government. Determined to do away with the old order, the revolutionaries, known as Bolsheviks, required new forms of architecture, design and graphics. A new movement known as Russian Constructivism was encouraged.

Designers such as Alexander Rodchenko (1891–1956) and El Lissitzky (1890–1941) used Modernism to create a new design style for the Revolution. Some of their most memorable work was in the creation of propaganda posters. This new graphic design used bold colour, and experimented with the way type was placed on the printed page. Type normally ran across the page horizontally, but the Russians began using words vertically or placing them at angles. They also redesigned the actual typefaces, or letter forms, preferring simple geometric shapes to the kind of decorative lettering associated with the nineteenth century.

Other countries shared the same language of Modernism but to different effect. In the Netherlands the movement was called De Stijl, and its designers, in the same way as the Russians, ignored decoration. Instead, they favoured simple forms, modern materials and, as far as possible, industrial techniques. They preferred the use of basic primary colours, such as the red, yellow and blue used by the Dutch designer Gerrit Rietveld for his famous chair, designed in 1919.

The chair was constructed using flat horizontal and vertical rectangles of painted wood. Part of its unusual appearance can be explained by the fact that it is trying to create a new idea of form for the twentieth century.

Another Dutchman, Marcel Breuer, designed a chair in 1922 that is still recognizable in present-day versions. This classic tubular-steel chair demonstrates another attempt to create a dynamic new form. Here, the designer has ignored any attempt to create traditional chair legs. The chair support is a continuous, shiny, streamlined tube of stainless steel and in itself, it makes an important statement of innovation and modernism. Sixty years later, versions of the same chair are still being produced for furniture shops all over the world, providing confirmation of its appeal as an example of modern design.

The enjoyment of machine images and geometric form had a wide popular appeal. After the 1914–18 war, a decision was made to hold

Right *William Van Alen's 1930 Chrysler Building is a much-loved feature of Manhattan's famous skyline. This photograph shows how effectively electricity could be used to light the tower at night in a most dramatic way. Sixty years ago this building was regarded as a marvel of new technology.*

Left *Mark Stam's tubular steel chair of 1926 has become one of the best-known chairs of the twentieth century. Its smooth and streamlined frame is a typical result of modern technology and mass production. This chair marked a departure from previous craft ideals of manufacture.*

Below *The Finnish architect and designer Alvar Aalto (1898–1976) designed this chair for use in a sanatorium in 1932. The distinctive curved shape of the seat is achieved using moulded plywood, and its simple sculptural lines have ensured the continuing popularity and production of this classic design.*

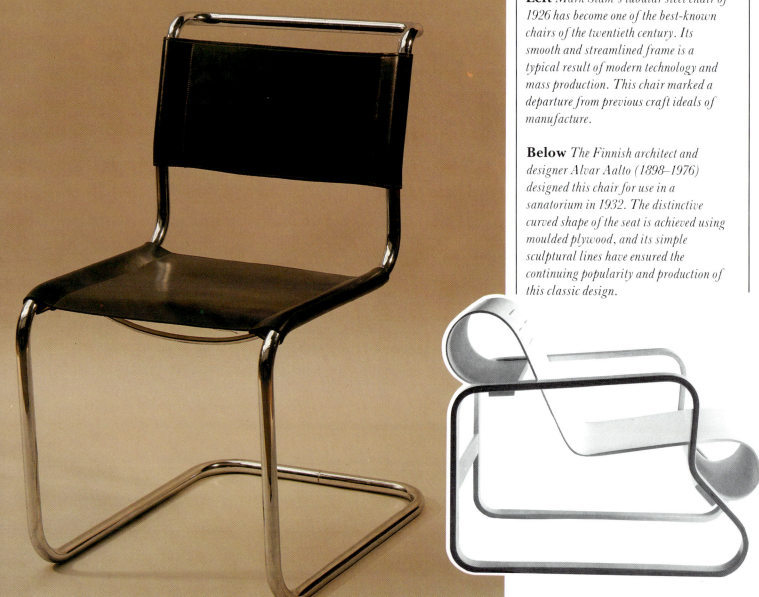

Above *This ashtray, decorated with a bronze figure, is typical of a whole range of domestic objects whose designs were influenced by the fashion for Art Deco.*

Below *Radio City Music Hall in New York is one of the most famous Art Deco buildings in the world. Inside the building the curved metal staircase, elaborate decorative panels and bold geometric lights represent the popular style of the 1930s.*

an international exhibition in Paris. It opened in 1925 and was called *L'Exposition des Arts Decoratifs*. From its French title came the abbreviated term Art Deco. This term is used by historians to describe the styles of many objects produced during the 1920s and 1930s, including cinemas, restaurants, and ordinary domestic objects such as light fittings and bathroom suites.

What these diverse products have in common are geometric forms, bright colour combinations, and a delight in futurist imagery. One of the best-known buildings in the Art Deco style is the famous New York skyscraper, the Chrysler Building, which is finished with smooth shiny reflective surfaces and shows a confident handling of many decorative elements.

Right *The Bauhaus design school
operated on limited funds. It had to
attract its students and sponsorship
through advertising and used posters such
as this to demonstrate its modern
approach. Note the way in which type is
placed vertically as well as horizontally
on this poster.*

STAATLICHES BAUHAUS WEIMAR 1919 1923

WEIMAR-MÜNCHEN

BAUHAUSVERLAG

Below *The famous German design
school, the Bauhaus, moved in 1925 to
this building in Dessau, which was
based on a design conceived by its
director, Walter Gropius. With its
adoption of large expanses of glass and
white concrete, this building epitomizes
the ideals of Modernist architecture.*

Art Deco as a period style can be seen everywhere. Local stores often have surviving shop signs from the period. Second-hand shops still sell items from the 1930s, and films of the period evoke the same style. Typical Art-Deco room settings and costumes can be seen in such films as the Fred Astaire and Ginger Rogers dance productions from the 1930s.

One of the most famous experiments in Modernism was a design school in Germany called the Bauhaus. The school was founded in 1919 by the architect Walter Gropius (1883–1969). Staff at this school tried to work out a new education programme for the teaching of design. So successful were the school's methods, that most contemporary design education is now based in some way on the Bauhaus programme. The school was only small and always short of money, but in the turbulent years of the 1920s and 1930s it attracted the great men and women designers of the period. Many of the names you will come across in books about the period and in museum collections of design, were connected with the Bauhaus school. These men and women include the architects Walter Gropius and Mies van der Rohe, the painters Wassily Kandinsky and Paul Klee, and the industrial designer Marianne Brandt.

The students and staff of the Bauhaus tried to work in cooperation with German industry and some of their designs for textiles, light fittings and graphics were put into production, creating world-wide interest. The Bauhaus, in theory at least, believed in the idea of a single style for design. It favoured pure logical geometric forms that rejected the ornate approach of the previous century. For some

26

designers, Bauhaus style became a very deeply held belief. By the 1930s, however, these ideas faced different problems. Europe was once again caught up in a major political crisis. In 1933, Adolf Hitler's Nazi Party came to power in Germany. The Nazis began to view the Bauhaus with increasing suspicion, suspecting that the staff might be members of the Communist Party, or might be Jewish. By 1936, most of the Bauhaus staff had fled from Germany, many seeking refuge in the United States, where they started new careers.

The Bauhaus contribution to American design was to prove an important one. However, in 1939 war was declared and new priorities took over. The struggle by the Modern Movement to create a dynamic new style for the twentieth century was not over, but now there were different problems to face.

Below *Classic Hollywood films can provide a wealth of period design in the detailing of clothes and interiors. This still from a Fred Astaire and Ginger Rogers dance sequence demonstrates the obsession with exotic glamour and symmetry that can be seen throughout the 1930s.*

When the Second World War broke out in 1939 it brought the production of ordinary consumer goods to a halt. People had to adapt to severe shortages which lasted well into the 1950s. Even the United States, by then the world's richest economy, had to deal with the problems of rationing. Many designers were called up for active service, although there was some design work that was regarded as essential for the war effort. Both sides looked to graphic designers to produce posters for recruitment and fund raising. In this way, designers contributed to the outcome of the war.

Below *Many museums reconstruct rooms from the past to illustrate how people lived. This British living room is dated 1953 and reflects the austerity of the post-war years. The sofa and the flying ducks are remnants of the 1930s, but the brightly-patterned modern rug suggests a new style to come.*

Right *This symbol was introduced by the British Government in 1941 to mark the beginning of rationing during the Second World War. The letters CC referred to Civilian Clothing and the scheme lasted until the early 1950s. The attitudes its use encouraged towards thrift and 'make-do-and-mend' affected a whole generation.*

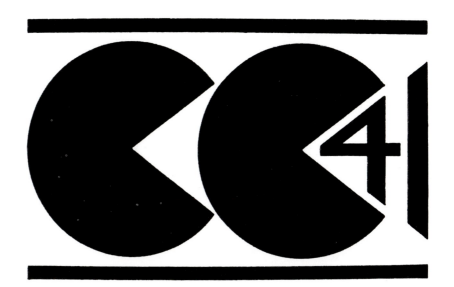

Throughout the Second World War, the shortages of materials and labour resulted, in Britain, in a scheme called Utility, which affected the design of such products as household goods, fashions and furniture. The design and pricing of Utility products were controlled by committees, which commissioned leading designers to be their advisers.

The Utility programme existed until 1953 and throughout that period, top British designers worked for the scheme. Famous couturiers, such as Norman Hartnell and Hardy Amies, designed clothes for ordinary consumers while designers of an equivalent high standard, such as Gordon Russell, worked in the area of furniture design. The Utility design-brief was restricted by the problems of wartime rationing. Simple extras such as decoration were prohibited, clothes had shorter skirts to save on fabric and a shortage of dyes meant that clothes and furnishings were rather drab and dull. Despite these restrictions, Utility helped to bring about important changes. Even such a limited contact with the country's best designers influenced people's expectations after the war. Utility helped to promote the idea that standards of living would eventually improve. Design was seen as a powerful way of bringing this improvement about and was to play a part in the rebuilding of Europe after 1945.

The United States played a significant role in this rebuilding process, providing funds for the defeated nations (Germany, Italy and Japan) under the famous Marshall Plan. Italy is an example of a country where design really expanded after the war. Defeated and demoralized, Italians looked to design to produce inexpensive, stylish goods for the home market and to boost exports. By the mid 1950s Italy had become a leader in this field. The famous Vespa scooter is one of the best-known examples. It was designed in the late 1940s as a cheap and cheerful form of transport but the scooter quickly became an international bestseller and is still regarded as a cult object.

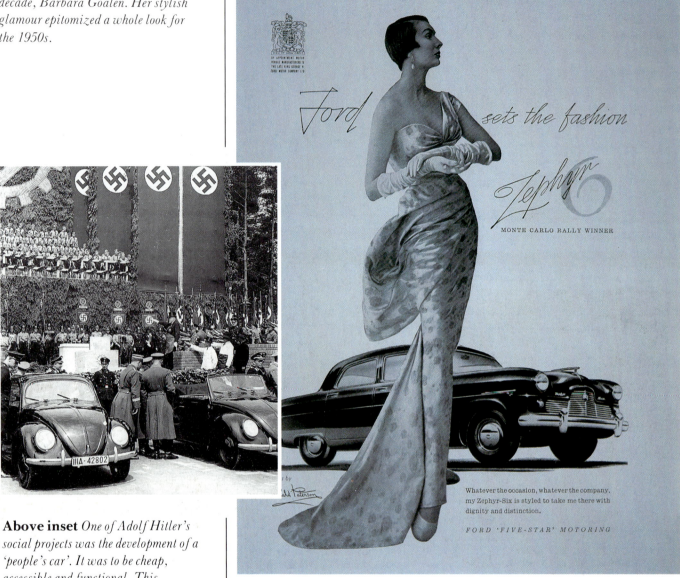

Right *This advertisement for Ford cars uses one of the most famous models of the decade, Barbara Goalen. Her stylish glamour epitomized a whole look for the 1950s.*

Above inset *One of Adolf Hitler's social projects was the development of a 'people's car'. It was to be cheap, accessible and functional. This photograph marks the opening of a production plant and suggests the value Hitler placed on this scheme. He felt that the car's development would bring him popularity, but in fact, the Volkswagen was not put into production until after the war, when it became an international bestseller.*

The design of cheap mass-produced cars also became important in the post-war period. Cheap cars had been pioneered by the American Henry Ford, and his Model T used the latest conveyor-belt methods of manufacture. Inspired by his example, European manufacturers tried to follow Ford's success in the 1930s and experimented with low-cost transportation. The best-known example of this ideal is the so-called people's car, promoted by the Nazi Party in Germany. The Second World War brought these experiments to a halt but efforts were resumed in the post-war years and, very quickly, Germany produced the famous Volkswagen Beetle. France designed the distinctive 2CV model of the Citroën, Italy the tiny Fiat 500 and in Britain, designers developed the comfortable rolling shape of the Morris Minor. The Morris Minor was designed by Alec Issigoni, who later, during the 1960s, designed the even more popular Mini. Only the United States chose a different approach to car design in the 1950s. At Ford and General Motors the priorities were rather different. Here, the 1950s were symbolized by massive consumer choice and cars were noted for customized details such as chrome tail fins and the use of bright colours, especially pink.

As well as designing popular items such as the Vespa scooter, Italy also took the lead in the design of certain fashion items, stylish accessories and shoes; the celebrated stiletto heel of the post-war period, for example, originated in the Italian footwear industry.

Like Italy, Japan had suffered enormous devastation in the war. Furthermore, it had been through the trauma of the world's first nuclear attack. Expertise from the United States helped to set up new industries to produce cars and electronic goods. Japan looked at the industrial West and set about building up her own companies. Soon Sony, Panasonic and Toyota were to become trading companies that

Below *This 1957 De Soto car sums up the American attitude to car styling during the 1950s. Wrap-around chrome bumpers, tail fins and vibrant pink bodywork represented a concerted effort by the car industry to win new customers and stimulate sales.*

John Armstrong 1947

were especially important for their production of electronic consumer goods such as televisions and radios.

During the 1950s there was a conscious attempt to mark the spirit of post-war optimism by creating a new design style. This style is often called Contemporary. It is recognizable by its use of new materials, mass-production techniques and distinctive shapes and colours. In this respect the war had been responsible for another development. During the conflict, government scientists on both sides were actively engaged in trying to invent new technology that would help their country to win the war. This research often resulted in important advances in design.

In the United States, for example, Charles Eames (1907–78), perhaps the best-known furniture designer of his generation, was working with the new plywood materials that had been developed for the construction of fighter aircraft. These materials were both strong and light. Eames took advantage of the new technology available to bend and shape plywood furniture into curving shapes, which were in some ways reminiscent of the sculptures of such modern artists as Henry Moore.

Eames, working with his wife Ray, went on to work for the important company Herman Miller. This company was determined to promote the new Contemporary look in the United States, commissioning not only Eames but the work of other important designers such as Harry Bertoia. These experiments were all part of the modern aesthetic principle of beauty. In varying forms, the Contemporary style appeared everywhere.

The Scandinavian countries played a major role in promoting the Contemporary style. In the 1950s they launched a series of international design exhibitions to promote their new post-war products. Scandinavian design used rich natural resources (such as their many varieties of wood), and strong craft tradition. Some of the

best-known industrial design products of the period came from such people as the Danish designer Arne Jacobsen (1902–71), who used dramatic tulip-shaped sculptural forms in his furniture.

Consumer demands in the 1950s were for cheaper and more elegant products for the home, and for an overall rise in the standard of living. Bright colour was also significant in the 1950s, as during the war dyes had been severely limited. Drab 'Utility' colours were now swept away and replaced by new sizzling colour combinations. Favourite colours included vibrant pink and orange contrasted with black and canary yellow. Cheaper and easier colour printing generated a boom for literature concerning home decoration, and the new styles encouraged daring mixes of colour and different patterns.

In Britain these design changes could be seen at a famous exhibition, called the Festival of Britain, which was held in 1951 to celebrate the centenary of the Great Exhibition of 1851. The Festival brought to the British people a taste of the new Contemporary style. Included was the spiky metal furniture of Ernest Race and new abstract-patterned fabric designs.

Britain also introduced another important aspect of post-war design. This involved promotion by official organizations. Design promotion also happened in other countries, including the United States and Scandinavia. In Britain the organization was called the Design Council and was set up to promote all aspects of design. Such organizations reflected the international trend of the time to promote Contemporary as the style of the 1950s. The same promotion of a single design style can be seen in the collection of the Museum of Modern Art in New York.

The promotion of a single design style is worth some discussion. In the late 1980s, our attitude is different and we accept that people can make any number of choices in design. Looking back at the magazines of the 1950s, we see that at that time, there appears to have been a single approach to design and the impact of Contemporary style was felt everywhere. In the 1960s, however, this began to change to meet the challenge of Pop.

Below *During the 1950s the Herman Miller Company made a determined effort to introduce contemporary design to the American market. Such leading designers as George Nelson created simple yet sophisticated furniture in the style shown in this reception foyer.*

Right *Charles Eames is probably the United States' most famous furniture designer. During the Second World War, he experimented with plywood in military designs, working on splints to transport the wounded. Eames utilized his knowledge of plywood in this 1944 chair design. Similar models were later manufactured by the Herman Miller Company.*

33

6 The Pop Aesthetic

The decade of the 1960s has become famous for its distinctive approach to design. This was the era of the miniskirt, pop music and social revolution. During these years the spotlight focused on London as the swinging city of new ideas. In 1964 the American magazine *Time* published a tourist guide to London for their readers. Detailed on this map were not famous historical attractions such as Buckingham Palace, but instead, the new fashionable boutiques of the Kings Road and Carnaby Street.

This was the beginning of a new style that is often described as Pop Design; a style that was directed almost exclusively towards the new demands of young people.

The most famous model of this period was Twiggy, aged fifteen, painfully thin and asexual in appearance. Her youth confirmed some of the priorities of 1960s society. The voice of young people became important. In the United States, students led the peace campaign against the Vietnam War (1959–1973) and became closely involved with the civil rights movement and the new spirit of women's liberation. It was a time of change, and design was no exception to these general attitudes.

During the 1960s Italian furniture designers were experimenting with new forms. In 1967 the design team of Lomazzi, D'Urbino and De Pas produced a Blow-Up chair in inflatable, see-through plastic. It was sold folded flat and inflated at home by using an ordinary car-tyre pump.

Ideas like this were intended to reflect the new lifestyles, which were not based around the traditional requirements of family life. They suggested fun, novelty and constant change. Products were often intended to have a very short life-span and there was a temporary craze for disposable products. One American company marketed cardboard furniture, which was packed flat and could be folded into simple, brightly-coloured shapes; this was rather like fast-food packaging but on a larger scale. This type of furniture was cheap and cheerful and when tired of it, you could simply throw it away.

Another famous Italian design was *Il Sacco*, or the Sag-Bag. This was a type of circular 'chair' sewn in cotton sections and filled with polystyrene pellets. It was cheap and easy to carry, and was moulded into a chair shape by the weight of the occupant's body. Once again its appeal was to the young and fit. Its design offered no support for the elderly, pregnant or disabled. Novelty, and the new lifestyles which seemed to be possible during this decade, were the priorities of much 1960s furniture design.

Right *Twiggy, pictured here in 1966 at the age of seventeen, was the most famous British model of the 1960s.*

Right inset *Designers during the 1960s enjoyed experimenting with new materials. This child's chair of 1967 is made from paper board and is cheap, disposable and fun. The decoration is made up of a brightly-coloured jumble of letters and numbers.*

Designers were also inspired by the promise of the new technologies that were developing in the 1960s. For the first time, computers were widely available and the United States was making tremendous progress with its space programme; in 1969, Neil Armstrong became the first man to land on the moon.

One of the effects of these developments was a great confidence in the role that technology was expected to play in the future. People began to talk about the world of the 1960s as 'a global village'. Many, in fact, thought that the technological revolution was going to happen much more quickly than it actually did. The idea of these changes can be seen in famous films of the period, from the hi-tech gadgets in James Bond films, for example, to the science-fiction visions of the future in such films as *Barbarella*, starring Jane Fonda.

Influenced by such attitudes, people began to admire a 'technological' look in the home. Plastic furniture began to be acceptable, as were the bold geometric patterns for fabrics and wallpapers, which looked as if they had come from a computer.

There were other influences on the look of 1960s design, in particular the work of Pop artists such as Andy Warhol. It was during this period that artists began to look at the ordinary elements of life, such as food wrappers, comics or advertisements, and to use them as inspiration for their art.

These everyday visual objects are often referred to as popular culture and they were felt by many serious critics to be insignificant. The new climate of the 1960s helped to change this opinion and artists and designers looked again at everyday images. One of the best-known examples of Pop Art can be found in Andy Warhol's multiple images of Campbell's soup cans. Paintings such as this invited people to take a closer look at their own culture and society.

Above *During the 1960s many products were re-styled to give them a Pop look. This picture shows a range of packages typical of the type of souvenir that was sold at this time. The sources of their decoration were comics, flags and Victoriana and they were printed in the bright and clashing colours then admired.*

Design captured the same theme, often using images from Pop-Art painter Bridgct Riley, for instance, for use in wallpapers and graphics. By the late 1960s this Pop influence could be found everywhere; on table-ware, clocks, clothes and in home decoration. Bold fluorescent colours in pink, green and blue were used together with strong geometric patterns.

At the same time, designers also enjoyed looking at anything that was slightly quirky or eccentric. Many enjoyed taking elements from the past, such as old advertisements, and using them in a new context.

Left *Psychedelia was a new fashion which appeared around 1967. In graphic art it led to surrealist, dreamlike images which were often dazzling in colour and pattern. Many people connected this style with the use of halucinatory drugs. This illustration shows artwork that was produced for the 1960s pop group, The Beatles.*

Below *The British pop group The Who, photographed in 1966 for the cover of the* Observer *magazine. They are wearing clothes designed by the Carnaby Street designer David English, who borrowed many style details from pop artists of the period.*

37

The cover of the Beatles album, *Sergeant Pepper's Lonely Hearts Club Band*, has the musicians wearing nineteenth-century military uniforms in 'day-glo' colours. It is a good example of the way in which all kinds of different sources were mixed together in the 1960s.

Design in the 1960s was an important issue for discussion and it even encouraged a new kind of approach to criticism. The American writer Tom Wolfe called this style the New Journalism. He tried to develop a fashionable, accessible writing style that made use of conversational slang, aiming at a direct type of communication with the reader. The title of one of Wolfe's books, published in 1965, *The Kandy-Colored Tangerine-Flake Streamlined Baby*, suggests the kind of literary style Wolfe used.

In the 1960s, design was optimistic, exciting and experimental. Its whole climate, though, depended on people's affluence and choice. Those elements had only ever been available to certain people in society, but with the coming of the 1970s they became available to even fewer people, as a new mood of caution was emerging.

7 Post-Modernism and Contemporary Design

One of the most important events to shape design in the 1970s was the oil crisis of 1973. It sparked off a world-wide economic recession, soaring inflation and massive unemployment. The crisis officially brought to a close the affluent, easy-going approach of the 1960s.

When we look back through magazines of the 1970s the style of the previous decade can still be recognized in the use of bold, bright colour and strong geometric form, but other, newer elements have also appeared. The severe economic problems the world was facing encouraged a restraint and caution that was reflected in a growing taste for nostalgia. During the 1970s, shops started selling items whose designs owed more to the ideas of country-living than to the reality of modern city life.

The success of certain chain stores such as Laura Ashley presents an example of this trend. Such shops sold furniture and clothes made from cotton materials, from designs that came from an age before the Industrial Revolution: for instance pretty bunches of flowers on white fabric, which were basically designs adapted straight from the fabrics of the eighteenth century. Soon, middle class families all over Europe and the United States began to buy objects, which we think of as traditional, to decorate their homes. Simple ceramic pots, dried flowers, hand-woven rugs and stripped-pine furniture became the new fashion. People bought the latest 'hi-tech' kitchen equipment and put it beside old pine cupboards filled with natural health products.

These new ideas are often described as the hippy culture. People actively sought out alternative lifestyles, extreme versions of which included moving out of the city and setting up communes. In general, social experiments such as these were idealistic but impractical. However, they did influence design. There was a new interest in different cultures such as Indian mysticism. Design details from the East began to appear in Western graphics and fashion, and during the early 1970s, pop stars such as Jimi Hendrix set the trend for wearing imported Indian clothes.

Trends like this reinforced the belief that the way forward for design was in opposition to the status quo. Victor Papanek, an important design theorist, summed up this approach in his book *Design for the Real World*, which was published in 1971. He argued that design should be more democratic and should be used to help to solve world problems such as starvation and disease.

Above *Sydney has a prolific creative community and is regarded as the centre of the design profession of Australia. The unique appearance of Sydney Opera House, built in 1959, has helped to create an international reputation for Australian design.*

Some of the ideas of alternative lifestyles were satirized in the contemporary novels and films of the 1970s. In 1976 the American novelist Crya McFadden wrote a book called *The Serial*, which looked at the lifestyle of one of the world's richest districts, Marin County in California. This novel provides humorous details about the extreme kinds of design people enjoyed.

Attitudes like this, however, were not merely fads. They came to have an important effect on the way we live now, and raised fundamental questions about the quality of our lives and environment. These new attitudes of the 1970s had an effect on architecture and design. Many designers looked at the buildings and objects designed after the war and did not altogether like what they saw. In particular they singled out for criticism the high-rise concrete buildings developed by architects eager to design new and exciting cities for the twentieth century.

Although these Modern Movement ideas were developed in the 1920s, they continued to have a powerful influence in the post-war years. By the 1970s, however, opinion about the importance of Modernism was divided. Many architects felt that the style was responsible for the inhuman atmosphere of contemporary cities. They wanted to look again at elements such as colour and decoration, which they felt had been ignored.

At the forefront of these new ideas were American architects and designers like Michael Graves and Robert Venturi. They put forward designs using details from the Classical past, such as columns and pillars, which were brightly coloured and had more than a touch of humour in their approach.

These new ideas proved to be both popular and controversial. Within the design profession, a fierce debate broke out about the direction in which design should progress. Critics called these changes Post-Modernism. The meaning of this word comes from the words 'post', (Latin for after), and 'modernism', the ideas of the Modern Movement.

Interesting and important design ideas came from Milan in Italy as well as from New York. Like other Western countries, Italy had suffered from the economic recession of the 1970s. Milan, once famous for new design ideas such as inflatable furniture, now became best known for the classic approach associated with the famous Italian company Cassina. This company produced superbly made furniture which was designed by such great designers as Vico Magistretti and Mario Bellini. Companies such as Olivetti used the same aesthetic for industrial design, with their wedge-shaped black typewriters.

The Italian tradition of good taste was challenged in 1981 by the appearance of a new Italian design group called Memphis. In the same way as the American architects tried to create new architectural forms, Memphis broke with tradition and produced a range of furniture that caused an uproar when it first appeared in the world's design press.

Led by a designer called Ettore Sottsass, Memphis furniture used bright nursery colours and bold surface patterns, which had a touch of the 1950s about them. Sottsass combined different materials, such as putting wood together with plastic laminates, normally only used for the kitchen. In this way he was challenging some of the conventions of design. As an example, he questioned why tables should necessarily have four identical legs. Instead he designed several examples with one supporting leg in the form of a classical column and with the others made from red plastic rectangles.

At first, people felt that the designs produced by Memphis were too extreme. They also thought that they were too expensive to manufacture and would never become popular. Almost immediately, however, Memphis had a world-wide influence on design. Memphis patterns appeared on advertisements and packaging; household goods like fridges appeared with Post-Modernist detailing; and new Japanese radios, made in bright pink and blue plastic, reached the high street. Influenced by a small studio in Milan, manufacturers all over the world exploited this new style during the 1980s.

Britain was another country that made an important contribution to the development of a contemporary style for the 1980s. Unlike the United States, however, where the pace was set by leading architects, or Milan, which was a centre for new design and industry, Britain's source of ideas was the world of popular music and teenage style. In

the late 1970s, a new youth-cult called Punk evolved in Britain. This movement had an approach to dress and music that has become instantly recognizable: pink spiky hair, torn clothes and aggressive looking make-up for both men and women. Punk was not only about the creation of a new street style. It possessed an anarchy and energy that was to have an important effect on design, particularly in the areas of fashion and graphics.

Graphic designer Jamie Reid worked on album covers for the pop group the Sex Pistols, creating a new style using torn-up letters and fluorescent colours. Soon other designers followed his example and started to experiment with the rules of graphic design. British graphic design became a very exciting area, encouraged by the new Romanticism of pop groups such as Culture Club and Bauhaus. Fashions had shifted from Punk to extravagant dress in the style of pop star Boy George.

Above inset *This unusual kettle and coffee pot were manufactured by Alessi. During the 1980s, this Italian company commissioned leading architects and designers to create a range of tableware with a new image. Aldo Rossi has here turned ordinary domestic goods into interesting design objects.*

Above *The Punk Movement became a powerful feature of British youth culture during the late 1970s. Punks adopted an aggressive approach to clothing, music and make-up. They became famous for their extreme approach to hair design.*

At the same time, new style magazines were set up, such as *i-D* and *The Face*. These reflected the new spirit of experimentation in Britain and by the mid-1980s, copy-cat versions of this style began to appear in New York, Tokyo and Milan. Food companies, banks, or anyone anxious to give their product a fashionable image, copied the colours, style and decoration of young British designers.

British fashion designers also caught the headlines with a new look that opposed the stiff formality of much French and American clothing. The best-known name in this movement is Vivienne Westwood, one of the founders of the Punk movement. Her styles were often outrageous and extreme, such as bras worn over dresses and socks which looked as if they had fallen down, but Westwood's ideas about the cut and detailing on clothes came to influence international fashion on the high street.

These ideas of rebellion and new forms for design also appeared in furniture. Aggressive metal furniture appeared, which often used re-cycled materials. The Rover chair by British designer Ron Arad re-used an old car seat and reflected a wider taste for experimental and quirky objects. Such designers added a touch of anarchy and originality to contemporary design.

Above *In 1981 the Japanese electronics company Sony launched a personal music system called The Walkman. It proved an immediate success and quickly became a cult object among both old and young people. Its creation was due to the wishes of the Chairman of the Sony corporation, Akio Morito, who wanted to listen to classical music during his frequent business trips.*

Left *Vivienne Westwood, famous for her Punk fashion designs, launched a series of successful Paris shows in the early 1980s. Shown here in her studio, . Westwood is now considered to be one of the most original fashion designers of her generation.*

43

Above *This table, Antelope, by the young designer Matthew Hilton, captures the spirit of the late 1980s.*

Below *The sleek and streamlined appearance of the Ford Sierra has helped to make it one of the most popular cars of the 1980s.*

Finally, it is important that we consider another element of design in the 1980s. Design as a subject has become very popular. As a word, it has entered the English language as a means of describing products. The term designer is now added to all kinds of goods, which include designer jeans. The word is often used as a way of adding some kind of extra value.

The media concentrates on design more and more and the number of exhibitions and books on the subject continues to grow at a fast rate. These developments reflect a developing interest in the subject of design and style.

In this book we have looked at the way design priorities have shifted since the Industrial Revolution, each generation trying to promote a single design style for the particular age. Design is now an exciting area and offers the individual many choices. The growth of financially accessible designer shops offer well-designed goods to the public at reasonable prices. In general, people have become more aware of the quality of design present in consumer goods and have begun to be more selective in their purchases. However, it is important to remember that even purchases made within a small financial budget are strongly influenced by design. The selection of items such as cassette tapes, chocolate bars and sweatshirts is highly dependent on the design of their packaging and the image which they try to portray. Many of the rules and conventions of style have been broken over the years and it is up to us as consumers to help decide the direction of design for the future.

How to See and Study Design

Only ten years ago there was very little media interest in design as a subject. Nowadays, however, there are frequent television and radio programmes on design, and the majority of national newspapers have a design correspondent. These correspondents treat design as an important cultural activity, and articles on the subject are found alongside pieces on art and the theatre.

General awareness of design and designers is also on the increase. You can see this for yourself by looking in any good bookshop or magazine stand. The number of titles that concentrate on the many aspects of design is quite considerable.

At the same time, many national governments have seen design as a way of increasing prosperity. In Britain, France and the United States there has been political support for design and public money has been invested to improve standards. These developments mark a change in attitude to design. Design and style have become important components in the understanding of our culture. The following sections make some suggestions about studying design in a period when the relationship between design and society has rarely been closer.

Further Reading

When you start looking for information you should use discrimination. Ask yourself who the book was written for. Is it, for example, a publication aimed at the serious collector or antiques dealer, or is it an academic text book for the university student? You can learn a great deal from reading the publisher's description of the book and the notes on the author. Make a note of when the book was written. A text on design written during the 1930s will reveal a very different set of attitudes from one written in the 1960s. The following is a selection of general books and dictionaries on design you may find in your library.

Careers in Design

Most design courses follow a simple structure. It is usual to do an introductory year, sometimes called a Foundation Course, which allows the opportunity to explore different activities. On a Foundation Course you will get experience of life-drawing and painting, as well as of work in three-dimensional forms such as furniture-making and sculpture. This broadening process will help you to choose the specialist area in which to train. Design offers many different areas in which to specialize: fashion design, theatre design, furniture design, graphic design, interior design, textile design.

Courses in these subjects usually take three years. To apply you must put together a portfolio of work to show that you have a facility for drawing plus creative ability in using colour and form.

Employment prospects for designers are generally good. It is a competitive business but most designers who leave college find work within a large design group. Alternatively they may work hard and set up on their own as independent designers. In recent years the status of designers has increased dramatically. In some countries, Italy, for example, famous designers are treated almost like pop stars, and this is a reflection of the new status of the design profession.

The Pioneers of Modern Design NIKOLAUS PEVSNER (Penguin, 1960) – a standard text, written in the 1930s, but frequently reprinted.

The Conran Directory of Design edited by STEPHEN BAYLEY (Octopus, 1985) – a comprehensive picture-book surveying design in the twentieth century.

Contemporary Designers edited by ANN LEE MORGAN (Macmillan, 1984) – a detailed index of modern designers; for reference only.

Industrial Design by JOHN HESKETT (Thames and Hudson, 1982) – an attempt to cover the whole area of industrial design.

Glossary

Aesthetic Artistic, or in some way relating to a sense of the beautiful. As a noun, this term refers to the set of principles underlying a particular style.

Anarchy Literally meaning lawlessness and disorder, when applied to design this term has come to mean creative disorder and the upturning of traditional values.

Art Deco A style of decoration, jewellery, architecture etc, which was at its height during the 1930s. It is characterized by symmetrical geometric shapes, which are often adapted for mass production. Art Deco objects also often used newly-discovered materials such as plastics and stainless steel.

Art Nouveau A style of art and architecture which flourished during the 1890s. It is characterized by flowing, sinuous outlines and stylized natural forms such as flowers and leaves.

Arts and Crafts Movement An artistic school of the late nineteenth century, which grew as a reaction to the effects of the Industrial Revolution. This movement inspired a revival of traditional crafts and a simple country style of design.

Autocracy A system of government controlled by an individual with unrestricted authority.

Capitalism An economic system which is based on the private ownership of the means of production, distribution and exchange of goods.

Classical Relating to, or characteristic of, the Ancient Greeks and Romans, or their civilizations.

Contemporary style The style that conforms to current ideas of fashion and design. The term Contemporary Design has also come to describe the campaign during the 1950s for modern style.

Couturier A person who designs, makes and sells fashion clothes.

Cult object An object (or style) relating to a popular fashion, which has been given a special importance.

Day-glo Fluorescent colours.

Entrepreneur A business executive who, by risk and initiative, attempts to make substantial profits.

Futurism An Italian artistic movement during the early part of the twentieth century, which replaced traditional aesthetic values with the characteristics of the machine age.

Genre Category or style, referring especially to an artistic work.

Graphics The process of art which is carried out according to mathematical principles. Graphic design has become a key branch of design and deals with the presentation of visual information.

Hi-tech A style which uses industrial products or design features for domestic use. This style became very fashionable during the 1970s.

Idyll An idealized version of rural life, as typified by pastoral and classically inspired painting and prose.

Imagery Descriptive language or a series of illustrations of a particular style.

International Style *see* Modernism.

Logo A symbol which is usually associated with a large corporation. Famous logos include those of Levi Strauss and Macdonalds.

Modernism (International Style) A style of design that was developed in the 1920s, shortly after the First World War. It was characterized by the use of new and experimental materials and plain and severe line. This movement has continued into the late 1980s.

Nostaglia In design, this term refers to a desire to echo or look back at the styles and events of the past.

Pop design Design based on the use of artefacts, advertising, mass media and the products of modern life. This style is typical of the 1960s.

Post-Modernism This term was invented in the 1970s to describe the contemporary architecture and design scene. This style includes a new interest in colour and decoration.

Prototype A model of a proposed design, which is normally made to show to prospective clients, from which changes can be made to the design.

Punk A youth style of the late 1970s, originating in Britain, which was characterized by brightly-coloured spiky hairstyles, torn clothes and an anarchic energy.

Socialism An economic system in which the means of production, distribution and exchange of goods are owned by the State.

Vernacular Relating to a particular trade or occupation, but in design this term refers to a tradition which has slowly evolved. A Windsor chair is an example of a vernacular design; the design has developed gradually over the years into its present-day form.

Index

Picture Acknowledgements

The publishers would like to thank the following for supplying the photographs for this book: Aldus Archive 6, 10 (bottom), 11 (top), 18 (right), 28, 33 (bottom), 35 (inset); Aram Designs Limited 24 (right); The Bridgeman Art Library 11 (bottom right), 12 (top and bottom), 14, 19 (left and right), 20 (right), 24 (left), 32 (top); Neill Bruce *cover* (courtesy of Jaguar Cars Ltd.); Cephas Picture Library 9; Chapel Studios 42 (top); The Design Council 8, 26 (top and bottom), 29, 36, 41; ET Archive 33 (top); Mary Evans Picture Library 7, 16, 20 (left); Ford Motor Company Limited 44 (bottom); Michael Holford 10 (top); Angelo Hornak Library 25 (left); The Kobal Collection 27; The Mansell Collection 18 (left); Peter Newark's Western Americana & Historical Pictures 5, 30 (right), 32 (bottom); Peter Roberts Collection 30 (left), 31; SCP 44 (top); Sony International 43 (top); Topham 4, 15, 21, 22, 25 (bottom), 35 (main picture), 37 (left and right), 38 (left and right), 42 (left), 43 (bottom); Josiah Wedgwood & Sons Limited 7; Zefa 40.